The Little Book of Practical Solutions

A Common Sense Guide to Understanding and Preventing Problem Behavior

Edward E. Hughes, MA

Copyright © 2006 NADD Press

 An association for persons with developmental disabilities and mental health needs.

132 Fair Street
Kingston, New York 12401

All rights reserved.

No part of this book may be reproduced, stored in a retrieval system or transmitted in any form by means of electronic, mechanical, photocopy, recording or otherwise, without written permission of NADD, 132 Fair Street, Kingston, New York, 12401

LCCN: 2006935704
ISBN: 1-57256-023-1

1st Printing 2006

Printed in the United States of America

Dedication

This book is dedicated to Ms. Gayle Oliver who taught me, as a young professional, that the promise and hope offered by behavioral psychology can never be fulfilled in the absence of compassion and caring.

About the Author

Edward Hughes has provided behavioral and mental health supports to individuals with developmental disabilities and their families for more than a decade. In addition, he has served as an expert consultant to state agencies and court monitors regarding the provision of behavioral and mental health supports. He has worked in private practice and is currently employed in Statesville, North Carolina, as the Clinical Director for Community Living Concepts, a community-based provider of supports for individuals with developmental disabilities and mental health needs.

Introduction

Over the years, hundreds of family members and support professionals have come to me for advice on how to help individuals with problem behaviors. I often wished I could give these folks a book that was written for them, not containing complicated jargon and cumbersome programs, but rather practical and effective support strategies. Unfortunately, although there are many books out there, I have never been able to find such a resource. Because of this, I have written *The Little Book of Practical Solutions.* This book represents my effort to provide families and professionals with the resource that I feel has been missing for far too long.

I have organized *The Little Book of Practical Solutions* into three chapters. The first chapter presents a model of how to understand the causes of problem behavior. The second chapter reviews the things we must consider prior to implementing behavioral supports. And, finally, the third chapter focuses on support strategies that can be implemented to help the individual with problem behavior.

As I wrote *The Little* Book, I attempted to ensure the support strategies and other information included reflected a positive person-centered approach to using behavioral principles with individuals with problem behavior. A positive person-centered approach recognizes each individual has a unique history and individualized interests and needs. This approach also recognizes that each individual experiences unique social, environmental, medical, and psychiatric factors that impact upon their life. Because of these facts, not all of the approaches described in this manual will be appropriate for every individual.

In keeping with a positive person-centered approach, I have tried to ensure the focus of the support strategies and information included in this manual is on increasing the individual's skills and abilities and on attending to the individual's desires and aspirations. More simply put, the goal of the information included in this manual is to ensure every individual is afforded the individualized supports necessary for them to have a satisfying life consistent with their desires and personal goals.

Although *The Little Book* may include all the information that is necessary to help an individual overcome their problem behavior, it must be recognized that there are times when the intensity, frequency, or complexity of an individual's behavior necessitates the involvement of appropriately trained professionals, such as a behavior analyst or a psychologist. Typically, if an individual's problem behavior results in the potential for harm to self or others, or is resulting in severe disruptions in an individual's daily life, it is advisable to involve professional support. However, if for any other reason you feel professional consultation is necessary, I strongly encourage you to pursue the involvement of appropriately qualified professionals

Involvement of professionals such as myself should result in a behavior support plan that includes a comprehensive assessment, interventions based on this assessment, plans for initial and ongoing training on the implementation of interventions, and data collection strategies to ensure interventions are achieving the desired outcomes. However, even in those instances where professional assistance is desired or needed, the information contained in *The Little Book* is of use as it will help you to be an active participant in the development of a formal behavior support plan. In addition, the information included in this manual should help you assess the appropriateness of any recommended interventions.

It is my sincere hope that after reading this book you will feel more positive about your ability to support individuals with problem behavior and, most importantly, that you will be able to make a positive contribution to the lives of these individuals and those who support them.

Contents

Chapter 1: Understanding Problem Behavior … 1

- Reinforcement … 3
- Triggering and Contributing Events … 5
- Putting the Pieces Together … 8
- One More Time … 8

Chapter 2: Getting Started … 11

- Medical Assessment … 13
- Mental Health Assessment … 16
- Signs and Symptoms That Something Is Wrong … 18

    Sleep … 19
    Appetite … 19
    Activity Level … 20

- Making the Referral … 20
- Getting Started … 21

Chapter 3: Support Strategies … 23

- The Importance of Communication: Setting the Tone … 25
- Environmental Contributors to Problem Behavior … 27
- Providing Choice and Self-determination … 29
- Individualized Behavior Support Strategies … 31

    Exercise … 31
    Improving Sleep … 32
    Dietary Modifications … 34
    Positive Mood Induction … 36
    Self-Monitoring … 37
    Relaxation Strategies … 38
    Art … 40
    Behavioral Contracts … 41
    Rule Rehearsal … 42
    Aromatherapy … 43
    Music … 44
    Problem Solving Dictionary … 45
    Sensory Activities … 46
    Verbal Strategies … 47
    De-escalation Strategies … 50

- Implementation and Monitoring … 52

In Closing	53
Appendix A: Behavioral Equivalents for Some DSM-IV Disorders	55
Appendix B: Tacking Sheets	65
Appendix C: Self Monitoring and Behavioral Contracts	69
References	77

Chapter One

Understanding Problem Behavior

All truths are easy to understand once they are discovered, the point is to discover them.

Galileo Galilei

To understand why the strategies in this book can be helpful in preventing and resolving problem behavior, we must first examine why these behaviors occur. Although you may be tempted to skip this section and jump to the chapter on support strategies, I strongly encourage you to take the time to read this part of the book. It will present a useful and easy-to-understand model of problem behavior that serves as the foundation for the support strategies you will read about later.

The model presented in this chapter is based on work done by Gardner, Griffiths, and Nugent (1999) and is the one I have used in my practice for over a decade. If after reading this section you would like more details, I suggest you read the book *Behavioral Supports: Individual Centered Intervention - A Multimodal Functional Approach* available from NADD.

Reinforcement

I'm sure we are all familiar with the concept of reinforcement. Reinforcement refers to something that happens after a behavior that increases the chances the behavior will occur again. There are two types of reinforcement, negative and positive. *Negative reinforcement* refers to the removal or avoidance of consequences the person finds unpleasant or unwanted. Because the unpleasant or unwanted thing stops after the behavior, the behavior is likely to occur again in the same situation. For example, let's say that every time you make a request of a person they have a tantrum, and because they are having a tantrum you stop making the request. If after a while you notice tantrums seem to be occurring more often - your removal of the demand (something unwanted or unpleasant) may be serving as negative reinforcement. Or, put another way, because something the person did not like (demand) stopped when they had a tantrum, tantrums continued or increased in frequency.

The other type of reinforcement, *positive reinforcement*, involves rewarding or positive things that follow a behavior and that result in an increased likelihood the behavior will occur again. For example, imagine a person is sitting by himself on a couch; he stands up, and then picks up a vase and throws it on the ground. This is followed by a lecture by the support staff about why the person should not have broken the vase. In this case, assuming that "breaking of vases" continues or increases, the positive reinforcement is the social attention (lecture) that was received by the individual after breaking the vase. Or, put another way, because something the person liked (attention via lecture) followed a behavior (breaking vase), the behavior continued or increased in frequency.

> **Reinforcement, positive or negative, is a consequence that serves to increase the frequency of behavior**

> **Negative reinforcement involves taking away something unpleasant. Positive reinforcement involves providing something pleasing**

It is important to note that reinforcement is individually defined. As such, things that are reinforcing to one individual may have a different effect on another individual.

If we develop a model of why problem behaviors occur, the action of reinforcement looks like this:

GENERAL REINFORCEMENT MODEL:

Problem Behavior + Reinforcement → Behavior Continues or Increases in Frequency

NEGATIVE REINFORCEMENT MODEL:

Tantrum (problem behavior) + Removal of demand (negative reinforcement) → Problem behavior likely to continue/increases in frequency

POSITIVE REINFORCEMENT MODEL:

Breaking vase (problem behavior) + Social attention (positive reinforcement) → Problem behavior likely to continue/increases in frequency

Triggering and Contributing Events

Just prior to problem behavior there is usually some type of *trigger* that signals the problem behavior is about to occur. You can often figure out the trigger for a given behavior by simply asking someone who observed the behavior, "What caused the behavior?" The response given usually relates to what happened just before the behavior occurred.

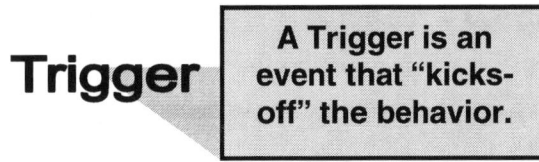

If we include this information, our model of how problem behaviors occur begins to look like this:

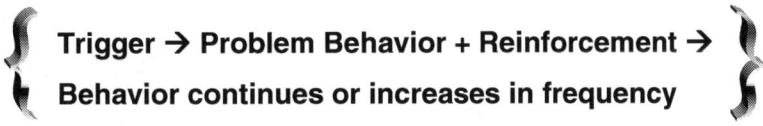

To continue with our examples, the trigger for the tantrum is the placing of the demand on the person. In the second example, the trigger would be sitting alone without any social interaction.

Presented another way:

Prompt (trigger) → Tantrum (problem behavior) + Demand removed (negative reinforcement) → Problem behavior continues

Sitting alone (trigger) → Vase broken (problem behavior) + Social attention (positive reinforcement) → Problem behavior continues

This however is not the entire picture, as there is often something else going on, whether we can see it or not, that causes the trigger to lead to the problem behavior. After all, to continue with the examples above, nobody has a problem behavior after every demand, or every time they are sitting alone. The key is determining why triggers instigate a behavior some of the time, but not at other times. In order to answer that question we must understand *contributing events*.

Contributing events are things that increase the chances triggers will lead to problem behavior. In the above examples, a contributing event for the tantrum could have been fatigue due to the person not sleeping well the night before. The contributing event in the second example involving the vase could have been that others received attention while the person sat alone.

Contributing Event | **A Contributing event is something that increases the chance that a trigger will "kick- off" a behavior problem.**

If we put all of this information together, our model of how problem behavior occurs now looks like this:

{ **Contributing Event (not causing problem) + Trigger (instigates problem when contributing event present) → Problem Behavior + Reinforcement → Behavior continues/increases in frequency** }

Or, using the above examples:

Fatigue (contributing event) + Prompt (trigger) → Tantrum (problem behavior) + Demand removed (negative reinforcement) → Problem behavior continues/increases in frequency

> **Others receiving attention (contributing event) + Sitting alone (trigger) → Vase broken (problem behavior) + Social attention (positive reinforcement) → Problem behavior continues/increases in frequency**

I should note that there are triggers that instigate problem behaviors without any contributing event being present. An example might be someone getting punched in the nose and then hitting the person back. You probably don't need a contributing event in such a scenario for the problem behavior to occur. However, the presence of a contributing event might increase the chances the person will respond with aggression rather than some other response. If we go back to our model of problem behavior, it might look like this:

> **Trigger (getting hit) → Problem Behavior (hitting back) 50% of the time. The other 50 % of the time the person responds appropriately (tells someone, walks away, etc.)**

Or, it might look like this:

> **Contributing event (crowded environment) + Trigger (getting hit) → Problem Behavior (hitting back) 75% of the time. The other 25% of the time the person responds appropriately (tells someone, walks away, etc.)**

In other words, the trigger can instigate the problem on its own, or the presence of a contributing event may increase the likelihood of the problem behavior after the trigger.

Putting the Pieces Together

Although reinforcement and triggering and contributing events have been presented separately, the reality is that these factors cannot be understood independent of one another. For example, simply knowing that an individual's problem behavior is continuing because of positive reinforcement is not sufficient in guiding us in developing a person-centered approach to helping the person. It is only when reinforcing events are understood in relation to triggering and contributing events that positive and effective person-centered supports can be implemented.

One More Time

Since we have covered a lot of ground in the past few pages, let's review. A *contributing event* is something that increases the chances problem behavior will occur. It, however, does not directly cause the behavior. A *trigger* is something that immediately precedes a problem behavior and may instigate the behavior on its own or in combination with a contributing event. *Reinforcement*, positive or negative, follows the behavior and increases the chances it will occur again.

$$\{ \text{Contributing Event} \rightarrow \text{Trigger} \rightarrow \text{Behavior} \rightarrow \text{Reinforcement} \}$$

If you want to test your understanding of the model we have been discussing, try to identify the contributing event, trigger, and reinforcing event in the example below.

A man diagnosed with mild mental retardation and schizophrenia believes his medicine is poison. When the nurse approaches him with his medication the man begins to hit his head on the wall. The nurse then backs-off and leaves him alone without attempting to get him to take his medication.

Contributing Event	=	**Belief Medicine Is Poison**
Trigger	=	**Nurse Approaching With Medication**
Reinforcement	=	**Nurse Leaves Him Alone and Does Not Try To Give Medication**

Chapter Two

Getting Started

In the observation of human behavior, one will notice every human act is a reference to a personal need.

Sidney Madwed

Treatment Approaches

The treatment of problem behavior usually consists of two approaches. The first approach attempts to remedy the behavior by changing what comes after it. The second approach attempts to remedy problem behavior by changing what comes before the behavior. As noted previously, however, only when these two approaches are integrated with one another can effective person-centered supports be provided. Given the general focus within the field of developmental disabilities on altering what comes after a behavior, and a relative lack of focus on what comes before the behavior, we will primarily review treatment strategies that are implemented prior to the problem behavior. However, the first step in providing effective behavioral supports is to ensure adequate medical and mental health assessments have been completed and all appropriate treatments are in place.

1 MEDICAL ASSESSMENT

As part of the process of implementing behavioral supports, the individual demonstrating the behavior should be referred for a thorough medical examination. This examination is extremely important because pain and discomfort can serve as contributing or triggering events for problem behavior. Research in the field of developmental disabilities is filled with examples of how discomfort associated with menses, constipation, ear infections, and allergies can lead to increased rates of problem behavior. Therefore, we should always ensure an evaluation is completed in order to rule-out medical problems that could cause discomfort and need treatment.

In addition to looking for undiagnosed medical conditions, the medical evaluation should also assess whether any medications the person is taking could be causing discomfort (e.g., nausea, dizziness) or psychological changes (e.g., depressive symptoms). Further, the medical evaluation should also include an assessment of the individual's hearing and vision to ensure deficits in these areas are not contributing to or triggering problem behavior.

If we go back to our model, the effects of medical problems or medication side-effects on problem behavior looks like this:

> **Discomfort due to menses (contributing event) + Prompt to clean room (trigger) → Aggression (problem behavior) + Demand removed (negative reinforcement) → Behavior continues/increases in frequency**

Or, we could see something like this:

> **Pain due to ear infection (trigger) → Hits self in ear to manage pain (problem behavior) + Pain lessens (negative reinforcement) → Behavior continues/increases in frequency**

As you can see, in the second scenario the discomfort caused by the medical condition (ear infection) served as a triggering event all by itself, as nothing else was needed for the behavior to occur. In the first example, however, a contributing event (discomfort due to menses) combined with the trigger (prompt to clean room) to produce the problem behavior. Although more rare, what we call problem behavior may be the direct result of a medical problem. For example, a person with temporal lobe epilepsy may engage in behaviors that we label as problem behavior (e.g., aggression), but occur as a result of neurological changes the person is experiencing due to seizure activity.

My experience, and probably yours as well, is that many individuals with developmental disabilities have undiagnosed or under-treated medical conditions. The latter point is significant in that we must not only ensure that medical problems are identified, but also that they are given appropriate treatment. These goals are not always easy to accomplish as there are a number of issues that may result in a failure to diagnose a medical condition or in an inaccurate diagnosis.

Barriers include the following.

- The initial presentation of a medical problem may be a change in the person's rates of problem behavior. For example, you may see an increase in a person's self-injury or aggression rather than hearing the person complaining about their ear.

- Uncommon conditions occur more often in individuals with developmental disabilities, and thus these conditions are likely to be misdiagnosed or missed altogether. Because of this, it is best to try to find a doctor with experience treating individuals with developmental disabilities.

- The individual may be unable to report symptoms or may be uncooperative with a physical exam.

Regardless of the challenges, medical evaluations must continue until everyone is certain that all possible medical contributors to the individual's problem behavior have been identified and addressed. If chronic medical conditions that result in ongoing discomfort are identified, we must ensure adequate pain management supports are in place. Pain management is important because pain creates anxiety, anxiety results in fatigue, and anxiety and fatigue can contribute to mental health problems. All of which may serve as contributing or triggering events for problem behavior. Pain management may include the use of over-the-counter or prescribed medication, but it can also include other approaches. For example, a physician may recommend relaxation techniques, exercise, use of heat and/or cold, distraction techniques (e.g., use of music), frequent periods of rest, or massage.

2 | MENTAL HEALTH ASSESSMENT

In much the same way that discomfort related to medical problems can contribute to problem behavior, mental health symptoms can also contribute to these difficulties. For example, irritable mood, a symptom of Bipolar Disorder, can serve as a contributing event for problem behavior.

If we go back to our model of how problem behavior occurs, the effects of mental health symptoms on problem behavior looks like this:

> **Irritable mood due to Bipolar Disorder (contributing event) + Taunt by peer (trigger) → Hits peer (problem behavior) + Taunting ends (negative reinforcement) → Behavior continues/increases in frequency**

Much like physical discomfort, symptoms of mental disorders can serve as triggering events. For example, you might see something like this:

> **Command hallucination to hit person (trigger) → Aggression (problem behavior) + Stress created by hallucination lessens (negative reinforcement) → Behavior continues/increases in frequency**

The importance of ensuring that mental health disorders are appropriately diagnosed and treated cannot be overstated. The available literature indicates individuals with developmental disabilities are at an increased risk for mental health problems. The available literature also reveals that people with developmental disabilities and mental health disorders are more likely to have problem behavior than individuals with only a developmental disability. Moreover, work in the fields of child psychopathology and developmental disabilities shows that problem behavior is often a symptom of an untreated, or ineffectively treated, mental health disorder.

Therefore, just as medical evaluations and treatment are integral to treatment for problem behavior, so too are mental health assessments and treatments. Recognizing and diagnosing mental health conditions in individuals with developmental disabilities, however, can be difficult. The primary barriers to the recognition of mental health disorders are that many individuals with developmental disabilities have limited communication skills and/or an inability to describe their emotions. Due to this, a number or professionals have recommended using *behavioral equivalents*, or easily observable behaviors, as a means of determining if symptoms of a mental health disorder are present. For your easy reference, Appendix A includes proposed behavioral equivalents for several of the more commonly diagnosed mental health disorders that can result in problem behavior.

Behavioral Equivalent

> A behavioral equivalent is the outward appearance or manifestation of a psychiatric symptom

How to Tell the Difference

It is often difficult to know whether problem behaviors are related to medical or mental health difficulties or are simply learned responses. Ryan (1999) provides some suggestions to guide us in determining whether a behavior is driven by medical or mental health difficulties or is a result of problematic learning. While there are always exceptions, I have found the following guidelines to be helpful. Specifically, Ryan suggests:

- If the behavior occurs in most or all settings it is more likely due to a mental health or medical condition.

- If the behavior has been unresponsive to consistent behavioral interventions and habilitative programming, it is more likely to be related to a mental health or medical condition.

- If there are autonomic symptoms (tremors, high pulse rate, sweating) at the time of the behavior, it is more likely the behavior is related to a mental health or medical condition.

- If the behavior seems to begin "out of the blue" or "all of a sudden" it is more likely related to a mental health or medical condition.

If it appears the behavior may be related to a medical or mental health condition, it is important to again consult with medical and mental health professionals to ensure all appropriate treatments are in place. In addition, it is important to remember that even though problem behavior may start as a response to medical or mental health issues, it can become so strongly reinforced over time that it may continue once the mental health or medical condition has been treated. Because of this, immediately assessing for and identifying and treating any medical or mental health conditions is extremely important.

3 SIGNS AND SYMPTOMS THAT SOMETHING IS WRONG

Medical and mental health evaluations can help rule-out medical or psychiatric factors as contributing or triggering events for problem behavior, but they tend to be one-time evaluations. If the person with problem behavior is not having difficulty at the time of the evaluation, medical and mental health difficulties may be missed. Additionally, the difficulties with language and communication experienced by many people with developmental disabilities may interfere with their ability to let others know that something is wrong. Therefore, it is important to be aware of changes in a person's behavior that may indicate they are having psychiatric or medical problems. If you notice a change in any of the behaviors described below, and there is not an obvious cause, the individual should be referred to his or her physician. If the physician is unable to identify a medical cause for the change in behavior, the next step would be to request a mental health evaluation.

The signs and symptoms to look for in determining that something may be "wrong" center on the person's sleeping patterns, his or her appetite, and his or her activity levels. Let's look at each of these variables individually.

a Sleep

The quality and quantity of sleep can have a dramatic effect on behavior and mental health. For example, poor sleep may lead to fatigue or irritability, which then can serve as a contributing event for problem behavior. Or, a lack of sleep can contribute to the development of depression, and the symptoms of depression (e.g., loss of interest) may serve as contributing events for problem behavior.

There are differences in the amount of sleep each of us needs to function best, but most of us sleep about the same amount from day to day. If a person is sleeping a lot less or a lot more than usual, or if their typical sleeping pattern changes, it may be a clue they are experiencing a medical or mental health problem. As examples, a person may not sleep much because of the discomfort caused by constipation or another person may experience early morning awakening due to depression. Again, the primary clue that something is wrong is that there has been a change in the person's normal pattern of sleep.

In order to determine if changes have occurred in a person's sleep pattern, you must keep regular data. Moreover, unless we consistently record sleep data it is difficult to assess the effectiveness of our attempts to help improve the person's sleep. See Appendix B for an example of a form that can be used to collect data on a person's sleep. This easy-to-use form can be filled out by the individual, by family members, or by support staff.

b Appetite

Changes in appetite can also provide a clue as to whether an individual is experiencing medical or mental health problems. One way to monitor appetite is by using food logs.

Food logs are daily journals in which we write everything the person eats and drinks. I don't typically recommend this approach, however, as it is cumbersome and time consuming and seldom gets completed consistently.

I have found that the most efficient way to assess for changes in appetite is to regularly monitor and document a person's weight. When significant weight change occurs for no obvious reason (e.g., increased exercise, going on a diet), there should be a strong suspicion that medical or mental health factors may be causing a change in the person's desire to eat. If unexplained changes in weight are observed, the person should be referred to his or her physician. If no medical causes are found, the next step would be to request a mental health evaluation by a psychiatrist, psychologist, or other mental health professional.

Activity Level

Like everything else, people have different activity levels. Most individuals, however, have a level that is normal for them. "Activity level" refers to how many things the person usually does during the day. This can include going to work, completing chores, working on hobbies, and the like.

If a person's activity level changes dramatically, it may be a clue there are unrecognized medical or mental health problems occurring. For example, a person experiencing pain due to arthritis in their knees may not wish to participate in activities that involve walking. Another example might include a person with Bipolar Disorder becoming much more active due to an episode of mania. Here again, the key is to recognize that a person's level of activity has changed from what is normal and that evaluation by a physician or mental health professional is indicated.

MAKING THE REFERRAL

If a referral to a physician is indicated, it is important to remember that we must be as specific as possible with the referral question. The more specific the questions asked of the physician, the more likely we will receive an accurate and helpful response. It is also useful to offer a brief description of what the person is normally like and then review specific changes that have been observed. For example, instead of simply asking for a medical "check-up", a better approach would be to ask the physician to evaluate possible causes for an individual's weight loss of fifteen pounds over the past four weeks. And, to share that while the individual has lost weight, he or she continues to eat one hundred percent of all of his or her meals and snacks.

5 GETTING STARTED

As you are going through the necessary processes to ensure all medical and mental health issues have been identified and appropriate treatments are being implemented, it is also important to identify other interventions that can have an impact on the person's problem behavior. The following chapter describes a variety of strategies that we can employ to help reduce problem behavior. None of the strategies described is likely to resolve an individual's problem behavior entirely. However, if several of the described strategies can be successfully implemented, we can make a positive difference in the person's life.

Chapter Three
Support Strategies

The only real failure in life is the failure to try.

Unknown

1 THE IMPORTANCE OF COMMUNICATION: SETTING THE TONE

The manner in which we approach others can have a significant impact on their feelings and behavior. If we are tense or anxious, the person we are interacting with is likely to become tense or anxious. Since tension or anxiety can serve as contributing events for problem behavior, we must try to ensure our actions do not create these feelings in others. On the other hand, if our actions contribute to positive emotions, these emotions can serve as contributing events for appropriate behavior. Therefore, it is always a good idea to keep the following in mind.

- **Begin your interaction socially**
  Spend some time chatting with the person about a reassuring topic (e.g., family, hobby) before asking them to do something or addressing a sensitive topic.

- **Use a non-demanding approach**
  Ordering or bossing others typically results in problems. Try a polite approach by asking rather than telling someone to do something, and don't be afraid to interject some humor into the situation.

- **Talk in a warm, easy-going, pleasant manner**
  Always use a tone of voice that you would like others to use with you.

- **Allow plenty of time for information to be absorbed**
  People with developmental disabilities or mental health problems may need more time to process and understand statements or requests. Allow a moment of silence before repeating statements or requests. Moving too quickly can cause frustration and decrease cooperation.

- **Keep the volume of your voice low**

    When people don't seem to understand us, we have a tendency to raise our voice. If we do this, it may cause the person to become anxious and actually interfere with his or her ability to understand what we are trying to communicate.

Let's review these points again:

> - **Begin your interaction socially**
> - **Use a non-demanding approach**
> - **Give choices whenever possible**
> - **Talk in a warm, easy-going, pleasant manner**
> - **Allow plenty of time for information to be absorbed**
> - **Keep the volume of your voice low**

If we ignore the issues identified above we can inadvertently contribute to problem behavior. But, by paying attention to the strategies noted above, we can help ensure that the stage is being set for appropriate behavior. Equally importantly, we can also be sure we are treating others with dignity and respect.

2   ENVIRONMENTAL CONTRIBUTORS TO PROBLEM BEHAVIOR

Before implementing treatment strategies for problem behavior, the places in which the behavior occurs should be assessed. When we evaluate the environment in which the problem behavior is occurring, we are looking for things that might be contributing to, or triggering, these difficulties. Features of the environment that may serve as triggers or contributing events include (Gardner, Griffiths, and Nugent, 1999):

- Noise
- Unpleasant smells
- Poor air quality
- Uncomfortable temperatures
- Poor lighting
- High humidity
- Limited space
- Cluttered furniture
- Crowding
- Uncomfortable furniture
- Limited activities
- Uncomfortable clothes
- Lack of privacy
- Violent individuals in environment
- Lack of choice
- Visual over-stimulation

Before you conclude there are no environmental contributing events or triggers for the person's problem behavior, it is important to ensure you have looked at the environment from the person's perspective. For example, an environment that seems perfectly warm to you may be experienced as quite cold by someone with Alzheimer's disease because of changes occurring in his or her brain. Or, a room that seems perfectly quiet and calm to you may be experienced as over-stimulating by a person with Autism or Fragile X. It is also important to be certain the environment has been assessed during the times the problem behavior typically occurs. After all, a room may not be hot at nine in the morning, but it may be quite uncomfortable at five in the afternoon.

In order to determine what aspects of the environment, as well as any other factors, might be contributing to problem behavior it can be helpful to keep a daily log describing the problem or situation. The log I typically use is called an ABC Tracksheet and includes the information described below. A copy of an ABC Tracksheet is included in Appendix B for your reference.

Antecedents (contributing or triggering events)

- What were the date, time, and place?
- What was going on just before the behavior?
- Who was involved?
- What was the emotional/physical state of the person and others present?
- What were the characteristics of the environment (e.g., loud, crowded, hot)?
- What were others in the environment saying or doing?

> **Antecedent variables (triggering or contributing events) can include people, places, things, activities, moods, etc.**

Behavior

- A thorough description of the behavior including frequency and intensity

> **The term behavior refers to an act or action that is the focus of concern.**

Consequences

- How did people respond to the behavior?
- How was the environment changed?
- What changes were noted in the person?
- Who was affected by the behavior?

> **Remember that consequences may serve as reinforcement for the problem behavior**

If there are factors in the environment that seem to contribute to or trigger the problem behavior, the first thing that should be done is to correct them. If they cannot be corrected, the person should be supported in changing their daily routine so as to avoid or better tolerate these things. For example, if the noise in the cafeteria has been noted as a contributing event for problem behavior, the person could be given the choice to eat lunch at a time when the lunchroom is less crowded and noisy.

In addition, if you notice that the person seems to always get the same thing after their problem behavior, it can help to provide the person free access to whatever that thing is. For example, if a person engages in problem behavior in order to get a drink of water, we could provide them with constant access to a water bottle. This is not a long-term solution, but it can be used in the short-term to ensure everyone's safety. Once the environment is safe, we can go about teaching the person other skills that will ultimately assist them in gaining the desired consequence in an appropriate fashion. To continue with the above example, this might include teaching the person to communicate they are thirsty or teaching them how to get a drink of water on their own. In any case, only after the environment is supportive of appropriate behavior should other interventions be implemented.

3 PROVIDING CHOICE AND SELF-DETERMINATION

Providing individuals with choice and control over their lives is a founding principle in person-centered planning, self-determination, and many other positive initiatives undertaken by families, self-advocates, and professionals over the past ten to twenty years. The promotion of choice and control is based on the belief that individuals prefer to have choices and that making choices for oneself has positive benefits. Research on this topic suggests that when individuals with mental retardation have choice and control in their lives they experience increased community integration, as well as increases in adaptive behavior. This makes a good deal of sense when we think about it. After all, if an individual has, for example, a choice in what they are going to eat for dinner, it seems logical they would be more interested in learning to prepare the meal.

The unfortunate reality, however, is that while much progress has been made in recent years, we still have a long way to go. More specifically, research continues to note that individuals with mental retardation who live in community settings are likely to have choice and control over common daily activities (e.g., what to wear, what time to go to bed, choice of leisure activities), but they generally do not have choice or control over some of the most important aspects of their life (e.g., where to live, where to work).

At this point you may be wondering what this has to do with providing behavioral supports. The connection is related to the fact that having choice and control in one's life can contribute to an improved overall quality of life. The experiences and emotions that result from an improved quality of life can serve as triggers and contributors for positive behavior and thus decrease the chances for problem behavior. Although choice and control must always be balanced with health and safety, we must strive, to the extent possible, to ensure that individuals with mental retardation are afforded the same opportunities for choice and control in their lives that each one of us desires. Some of the ways we can encourage choice making and self-determination include:

- Offering choices during all daily activities
- Respecting others' choices even when they are not the decisions we would have made
- Providing positive feedback when people make choices
- Avoiding "ordering" or "bossing" others
- Avoiding unnecessary confrontations
- Assisting individuals in recognizing the various possible choices available to them
- Helping individuals understand the consequences of different choices

4   INDIVIDUALIZED BEHAVIORAL SUPPORT STRATEGIES

a. Exercise

The use of exercise is a well-established means of improving mood, reducing tension, and relieving anxiety. Regular exercise has also been shown to lower blood pressure, relieve constipation, enhance pain tolerance, decrease muscle tension, and improve sleep. By reducing the occurrence of medical problems, tension, and anxiety, any of which may serve as contributing or triggering events for problem behavior, the likelihood of problem behaviors is reduced. Conversely, the benefits of exercise, such as improved mood, can serve as a contributing or triggering event for positive behavior.

When using exercise as an intervention for problem behavior, the following should be kept in mind.

- Exercise has immediate effects such as mood improvement, muscle relaxation, and anxiety reduction for the hour or so following exercise. Because of this, it may be useful to encourage folks to exercise prior to activities that usually contribute to problem behavior. After all, if you are in a good mood or relaxed, you are less likely to have difficulties.

- Exercise has long-term effects such as improved mood stabilization and lowered reactivity to stress. Therefore, even if you do not see immediate effects of exercise on problem behavior, don't give up, the effect may only occur after four to six weeks of consistent exercise.

- Mild-to-moderate exercise, such as walking, can be just as effective as high-intensity aerobic exercise.

- Minimally, exercise should occur three to four times a week for twenty to thirty minutes.

When I have suggested to individuals that they exercise more frequently, I have usually received a less than enthusiastic response. In order to get individuals to exercise regularly we often need to incorporate the activity into a social or leisure activity (e.g., going to the gym, playing basketball in a league, etc.). Another way to increase cooperation is to encourage the person to develop an "activity partner" with whom the person regularly exercises. Here again, the idea is to take the focus off exercising and emphasize the enjoyable social component. Remember, even if exercise does not directly contribute to reduced problem behavior, it may lesson the chances of future medical or mental health problems that could contribute to such behavior.

Before encouraging an individual to exercise, be sure to consult with a physician first. This is extremely important as individuals with certain medical conditions may have limitations regarding how much, and under what conditions, they should exercise.

Sleep

The impact of inadequate or poor sleep on an individual's problem behavior can be significant. Research has shown that sleep disturbances can contribute to problem behavior. Some researchers believe that problem behavior occurs, in part, because of the fatigue and irritability caused by sleep disturbances. Think about it, how grouchy and tired are you after a couple nights of not sleeping well. Inadequate sleep has also been noted to contribute to the development of mental health disorders like depression. Because of this, if an individual is having problem behaviors, it is important to ensure that he or she is getting a good night's sleep.

When attempting to help someone improve his or her sleep, we should try to keep in mind the following (Preston, 2001):

- While regular exercise can help improve a person's quality of sleep, it needs to occur earlier in the day. Ensure that moderate to intense exercise does not occur in the two to three hours before bedtime. The reason for this is that exercise is an arousing activity and heightened arousal can interfere with some individuals' sleep.

- Bright light and noise can stimulate the brain and thus they should be avoided in the later parts of the evening. It may be helpful to dim the lights and play soft music one to two hours before bedtime.

- A common source of entertainment in the evening is watching television or movies and playing video games. However, exciting television programs (e.g., sporting events) and movies (e.g., action movie) should be discouraged late in the evening. Exciting or tension producing video games should also be discouraged. Rather, interesting but more calming activities should be encouraged (e.g., playing solitaire, looking at a magazine, etc.).

- The impact of diet will be discussed in more detail later, but for now I will just note that late-evening snacks consisting of primarily protein, without carbohydrates, can increase arousal and interfere with sleep. Thus, this type of late night snack should be avoided. A more advisable late night snack would be a light carbohydrate snack with a warm glass of milk.

- Caffeine should be eliminated from a person's diet. Consumption of more than 250 milligrams of caffeine, approximately 12 ounces of coffee or 60 ounces of soda, can have a significant impact on a person's quality of sleep. Caffeine, even if it does not keep a person awake, can diminish deep sleep. This fact is important because deep sleep is the type of sleep needed to ensure you feel rested upon awakening.

- Attention must also be paid to medications as some actually include caffeine (e.g., Midol, Excedrin, Dristan). Also, medications like antidepressants may increase the time caffeine spends in the bloodstream and thus small amounts of caffeine may have a larger impact than expected. Always check medication labels and side-effect listings and then discuss any concerns with the person's physician.

Other things that can be done to enhance sleep include:

- Using the bed only for sleep
- Taking a warm bath or shower prior to bedtime
- Engaging in the same routine just before going to bed
- Avoiding daytime naps
- Encouraging the person to use the bathroom prior to going to bed
- Providing night-lights or soft lighting in the person's bedroom
- Playing soft music, nature sounds (ocean surf), or using a white-noise machine to block out sounds that might wake the person during the night

If the above strategies do not seem to make a significant difference, it may be wise to assist the individual in approaching their physician and requesting a sleep study. As an example of how important this might be, I used to work with a gentleman who had a long history of serious problem behavior. Due to reports that he was not sleeping well, as well as the fact that he was overweight and snoring, his physician ordered a sleep study. The study found that he had sleep apnea. Once his sleep apnea was treated, his rate of problem behavior dropped to almost zero and he was much happier. While the treatment for sleep apnea was not the only support being implemented, it was clear that without treatment for this issue, the other supports were never going to be as effective as they could be.

C Dietary Modifications

Changes in a person's diet may have an impact on problem behavior through the effects of diet on fatigue and anxiety. Fatigue and anxiety, of course, are two factors that can serve as contributing or triggering events for problem behavior. For some individuals, the dietary modifications about to be discussed may have a dramatic effect. For others, there may be no noticeable effect. Before attempting dietary changes, the person's nutritionist or physician should be consulted to rule-out any negative consequences of using this strategy.

Getting Rid of Anxiety

Dietary control of anxiety is based on the fact that anxiety generally decreases with increases of the neurotransmitter serotonin. This is a bit complicated so let's review how serotonin is made. The amino acid that serves as the building block for serotonin is tryptophan. Most of us have adequate supplies of tryptophan in our bodies, so the trick is ensuring the tryptophan can get into the brain so it can be turned into serotonin. This can be accomplished by increasing insulin levels.

You can increase insulin levels by eating carbohydrates. More specifically, snacks or meals should include low-sugar carbohydrates like that in beans, peaches, apples, bran, pears, grapes, plums, and oranges. Although simple carbohydrates like sugars can produce a temporary improvement in mood, they are not recommended because most folks experience a "sugar crash" that ultimately causes an intensification of anxiety. And this anxiety can then serve as a contributing event or trigger for problem behavior.

Getting Rid of Fatigue

One way of relieving fatigue is to increase the levels of the neurotransmitters dopamine and norepinephrine. The building block for both of these brain chemicals is tyrosine. Therefore, protein, which includes the amino acid tyrosine, can be used to increase alertness and energy. This is actually a strategy used by the US military to improve the alertness of pilots while they are flying long missions. In order for this to work, the protein must be eaten alone or with very small amounts of carbohydrates. Some of the best sources of protein include protein-powder, eggs, fish, chicken, American cheese, and beef.

An example of how this can work comes from a young man with whom I used to work. This gentleman was always very lethargic in the morning and his lethargy (contributing event) combined with prompts to complete his morning activities (trigger) often led to problem behavior. In addition to ensuring he was getting adequate sleep, he was offered a protein bar first thing in the morning. This helped to reduce his fatigue and thus a contributing event for some of his problem behavior was eliminated.

Positive Mood Induction

I assume it comes as no great shock to learn that when people are in a bad mood they are more likely to have problem behavior. Much in the same way that a bad mood can serve as a contributing or triggering event for problem behavior, a good mood can contribute to appropriate or positive behavior. Recent research (Carr et al., 2003) seems to prove that providing individuals with frequent mood enhancing activities can decrease the chances of problem behavior.

Unfortunately, participation in mood improving activities often decreases as problem behaviors begin to occur. This usually results from a drift towards punishment and restrictions as our frustration with the person's problem behavior increases. This drift may ultimately lead to increased problem behavior due to an unintentional decrease in the number of mood-enhancing activities in a person's life. Thus, to ensure the person has the opportunity to participate in mood-enhancing activities, I recommend the following steps.

>**Step One:** Gather people who know the individual well and ask them "What would you do if you had to put this person in a good mood right now?" Obviously, it is also important to ask the person what things he or she enjoys doing. Write all of the thoughts down for future reference.
>
>**Step Two:** Get a calendar and schedule as many of the activities identified in Step One as possible. This may seem like overkill, but the goal is to help the person stay as active in mood-enhancing activities as possible. This approach is especially effective if you schedule these activities for the times of day the person typically engages in problem behavior. Thus, instead of engaging in problem behavior during a time of day associated with these behaviors, the person is doing a fun activity that puts him or her in a good mood that contributes to positive behavior.
>
>**Step Three:** Ask the same people you asked in Step One "What would you do if you had to put this person in a bad mood right now?" Again, remember that it is

extremely important to also ask the person what puts him or her in a bad mood. Again, write all of these thoughts down for future reference.

Step Four: To the extent possible, help the person adjust his or her life so as to minimize the occurrence of any activities or events identified in Step Three. If the activity or event that contributes to a bad mood cannot be avoided; try to ensure activities and events from Step One (mood-enhancing activities) are scheduled just before or just after the disliked activity. Doing so may help the person better tolerate the non-preferred activity and thus decrease the chances for problem behavior.

By increasing the frequency of mood enhancing activities and decreasing the frequency of activities that result in a bad mood, we can have a significant impact on problem behavior. We can also support a person in having a more satisfying lifestyle.

Self-Monitoring

Self-monitoring involves observing one's own behavior and recording when a specific behavior is displayed. The simple act of recording a self-observed behavior has been shown to result in a change in the occurrence of unwanted behavior (Barry and Messer, 2003). This may sound too simple to be true until you think of how many of us have used this strategy in our lives. I'm sure at least some of us have charted our weight on the refrigerator to self-monitor our eating habits or counted how many cigarettes we smoked to help us cut back. Although much of the focus of self-monitoring has been on identifying and recording problem behavior, the strategy can also be used simultaneously or by itself to identify and self-monitor desired behavior. This type of self-monitoring then leads to an increase in desired behaviors. The benefits of self-monitoring, besides helping to change a person's behavior, are that it helps the individual to develop internal control of their behavior and requires little supervision and effort by support staff or family members.

The first step in teaching self-monitoring is to help the person, through a verbal review or modeling, to identify and record the desired behaviors. A verbal review involves simply talking about the behavior while modeling involves acting out behaviors and having the individual discriminate between the target behavior and other behaviors. The goal of these activities is to ensure the person understands which behaviors are being monitored. Once this is accomplished, the individual should be supported in rehearsing the behavior and self-recording.

The process of self-monitoring may involve anything from making checkmarks on a data sheet to using a wrist-counter to moving poker chips from one pocket to another. The tool used for self-monitoring should be portable so the desired behaviors can be documented as they occur. It is also effective, however, to use self-monitoring systems that consist of evaluating the occurrence of specific behaviors at set times or places during the day. For example, a person living in a group home may evaluate their behavior during each shift change. Having set times during the day for someone to self-monitor their behavior is often preferred because the person has usually calmed down and is more open to thinking about, and admitting to, any problem behavior he or she may have displayed. Examples of some of the types of self-monitoring tools I have used in the past are included in Appendix C.

f. Relaxation Strategies

The use of calming or relaxation techniques is an often-overlooked strategy in helping to prevent problem behavior. The teaching of calming strategies really serves one purpose. That purpose is to help the individual self-manage stress, tension, or anger, all of which may serve as contributing or triggering events for problem behavior. Relaxation strategies are also effective because they distract the person from the source of the stress and focus them on an appropriate behavior.

Although progressive muscle relaxation is often advocated and is a great relaxation strategy, I have found that it tends to be too complicated for most individuals with developmental disabilities or significant mental health needs. Therefore, I tend not to recommend progressive muscle relaxation, but I have found that the following more simple strategies can be effective in assisting folks with relaxation and calming:

RELAXATION/CALMING STRATEGIES

Fist Clenching:
1. Clench fists as tight as possible
2. Hold for about four seconds
3. Let go and let entire body go limp
4. Repeat 3-5 times

Counting:
1. Breathe normally
2. Count backwards from 10-0 with one number on each breath
3. Take a deep breath and exhale

Breathing:
1. Take a full deep breath
2. Hold to count of four
3. Slowly exhale while counting or saying "relax"
4. Repeat 3 times

Pillow Hug:
1. Place a pillow against chest
2. Squeeze tightly for 4 seconds
3. Release pillow and let entire body go limp
4. Take a deep breath and exhale
5. Repeat 3 times

Deep Breathing:
1. Sit or lie down
2. Place one hand on stomach
3. Breath in slowly through the nose and try to ensure the stomach rises
4. Slowly exhale while counting or saying "relax"
5. Repeat 3 times

For any of the above strategies to be effective when the person is agitated or anxious, the strategies must have been practiced regularly when the person was calm. After all, the time to teach someone something new is when he or she is receptive to it and able to learn.

Another way to help individuals relax is to encourage them to take a warm bath or shower. Since this is not a strategy that typically works once someone is engaging in problem behavior, the best plan is to encourage the person to take warm baths or showers several times a day or at early signs of distress. This helps promote overall relaxation (contributing event for positive behavior) and also decreases the chances the person will become tense or stressed (contributing events for problem behavior). While taking several baths or showers a day may not seem all that practical, given the amount of disruption that problem behaviors can create the benefits may very well outweigh any inconveniences.

If you decide to use frequent warm baths or showers to promote relaxation, be aware that warm baths may contribute to dry skin. This is important as itching and discomfort due to dry skin could serve as a contributing event for problem behavior. I typically check with the person's physician prior to using this approach and always advocate for the use of moisturizing lotion.

Art

Art therapy, unlike your typical art class, is focused on the creative process involved in creating art – not the art that is ultimately produced. Research in the area of art therapy indicates that the benefits include positive self-esteem, reduced anxiety, and improved self-expression (Stamatelos and Mott, 1985). These benefits are important because low self-esteem, anxiety, and an inability to express oneself can all serve as contributing or triggering events for problem behavior.

If possible, it is best to enlist the services of an art therapist to work with the individual with problem behavior. Unfortunately, art therapists can be quite difficult to find. My experience, however, is that art can still help individuals reduce their problem behavior, even when used outside of formal therapy. The use of art outside of formal therapy is actually quite similar to unstructured art therapy. This form of art therapy involves encouraging individuals to choose which materials to use and what subject matter to focus on.

So, now that we know all of that, what next? The first step, if an art therapist is not available, is to expose the person to a hands-on art class at a local community college, art studio, craft store, etc. If such classes are not available, the next best approach is to provide the person with a variety of art media (e.g., paint, clay, charcoal, etc.) with the hope of finding several media in which the person is interested. Once media are identified, the person should then be provided with free access to the materials and be encouraged to use them frequently. Remember, the technical merit of the art is not important. Rather, what matters is that the person learns how to express his or her emotions through non-verbal means.

The regular use of art can help the person with problem behavior express his or her emotions, lower anxiety, and improve mood. All of these then can serve as contributing events for appropriate behavior. Art can also be used to avert problem behavior by encouraging the person to use their art materials when early signs of distress or agitation (contributing events for problem behavior) are observed. But remember, never give an agitated individual access to art materials that could be used to harm themselves or others (e.g., paint knife) or that are likely to be ingested by the person.

h. Behavioral Contracts

Behavioral contracting is a strategy used to structure an agreement between two individuals. The contract is a written agreement that specifies behaviors to be engaged in or refrained from during a specified period of time (e.g., 24 hours, one week). If the person cannot read, pictures or drawings can be used to help the person understand the nature of the agreement. The contract further specifies the reinforcement that will be provided when the person meets the expectation included in the contract. The contract can also be used to specify penalties for engaging in problem behavior.

When I use behavioral contracting, I always include a self-monitoring component. I also like to ensure the contract specifies behaviors the person should engage in, such as a calming strategy, as well as the problem behavior the person has agreed not to display. I generally try to address only one or two problem behaviors in the contract. I limit the contract to just a few behaviors because one of the goals of behavioral contracting is for the person to achieve success and obtain reinforcement. This goal is difficult to achieve if we overwhelm the person with goals they can never meet.

When addressing a problem behavior that is occurring at a high rate, I will sometimes structure the contract so the person can display low rates of the problem behavior and still obtain the reinforcer. For example, if a person averages twelve incidents of problem behavior a day, the contract may require the person to engage in nine or less incidents a day. Once the person is regularly meeting the goals in their contract, the contract is usually renegotiated and lower rates of problem behavior are then required to earn the reinforcer. Examples of behavioral contracts are included in Appendix C to give you an idea of how these can be structured.

Rule Rehearsal

A rather simple but effective way to help an individual refrain from engaging in problem behavior is to regularly review the rules of conduct with him or her. When I use this strategy, I typically schedule the rule rehearsal so that it occurs just prior to any activities or times of day that are regularly associated with problem behavior.

Rule rehearsal consists of reviewing the rules of expected behavior with the person who has the problem behavior. The rules can be reviewed verbally, in writing, or through pictures depending on the needs of the individual. To the extent possible, the rules should be presented in such a way as to inform the person of things they should do versus what they should not do. For example, it is better to present a rule as "I will use my calming strategy when I am upset" rather than "I will not hit." If the person has a behavioral contract, the rule rehearsal can consist of simply reviewing this contract. The review of behavioral expectations should always occur in private so as not to embarrass the individual or violate his or her right to confidentiality.

The purpose of rule rehearsal is two-fold. First, this strategy helps teach people which behaviors are expected or are acceptable and which are not. Second, this strategy regularly reminds and orients the person to the expected behavior. I have found the latter point is quite significant and can have a noticeable impact on behavior. After all, if someone reviewed the speed limit and the consequences of speeding with you every time you got in the car, you would probably be more aware of and compliant with the posted limit – wouldn't you?

J Aromatherapy

Aromatherapy is the practice of using essential oils to promote health and well-being. Advocates of aromatherapy claim essential oils stimulate the olfactory nerve, which sends signals to the limbic system in the brain. Because the limbic system influences emotions, and emotions can serve as contributing or triggering events for problem behavior, aromatherapy has a place in helping individuals with problem behavior. Specifically, research demonstrates aromatherapy can have a significant impact on the levels of agitation displayed by people with dementia. Aromatherapy combined with a hand massage has also been shown to decrease agitation in individuals with dementia (Smallwood et al., 2001) and to lower anxiety in patients undergoing medical procedures (Hadfeild, 2001). Medical benefits such as lowered blood pressure are also noted in the literature. Additionally, one of the advantages of aromatherapy is that support staff and family members also benefit from the therapy when they are in areas where aromatherapy is administered.

Some of the essential oils researchers have suggested to reduce anxiety and agitation include:
- Essential oil of Melissa officinalis (lemon balm)
- Essential oil of Roman chamomile
- Essential oil of Lavender
- Essential oil of Rosewood
- Essential oil of Citronella
- Essential oil of Eucalyptus

There are several ways to use essential oils for the purpose of aromatherapy. The oil can be applied like a perfume, it can be added to a warm bath, or it can be added to a base lotion. The oils can also be dispensed into the air by spray mists or through the use of a diffuser. My experience is that aromatherapy can be quite effective for some individuals, if you can convince skeptics to give it a try.

Before using aromatherapy with an individual, be sure to consult with a physician first. This is extremely important as individuals with certain medical conditions should not be exposed to essential oils and others may be allergic. Also, be aware that essential oils can be flammable and may be harmful if ingested. Therefore, essential oils should be stored in a safe place away from fire hazards and where individuals who might swallow them cannot access them. If you choose to use essential oils, always be sure to follow the manufacturers' recommendations regarding appropriate use and safety precautions.

Music

Music can have a significant effect on a person's mood or emotional state. This probably comes as no surprise as most of us have had the experience of music changing our mood. Who, after all, has not teared-up while listening to a particularly sad song on the radio? The ability of music to change mood is important because mood can serve as a contributing event for either problem or appropriate behavior.

Research involving the use of music to change mood has shown that music can be used to help individuals calm once they have become upset. Gardner (2000) found this to be true with individuals with dementia. I have found that music can also be used to establish emotional states or moods that can contribute to appropriate behavior. The use of music is often a good choice as an intervention because it is non-invasive, inexpensive, safe, and easily administered. Also, staff or family members working with the individual can benefit from the therapy as well.

What all of this means in practical terms is basically two things. One, calming music can be used to prevent problem behavior when it is played at the initial signs of agitation or impending problem behavior. Second, the regular use of calming music can be used as a contributing event for positive behavior thereby decreasing the chances of problem behavior. Again, I generally try to enhance the potential positive effects of music by playing it during the times of day or during the activities usually associated with problem behavior.

You may be wondering what type of music works best. Well, the use of classic "relaxation" music has been shown to have a positive effect on problem behavior and can be purchased at most large multi-media stores. Designer music such as *Medical Resonance Therapy Music* by Peter Hubner and *Speed of Balance* composed by Doc Childre has many advocates who affirm its efficacy in decreasing stress and increasing relaxation. I have also found that predictable and rhythmic nature sounds, such as ocean waves, work well. Caution must be used, however, if you decide to use nature sounds since unpredictable sounds (e.g., birds chirping) are usually arousing rather than calming.

Problem Solving Dictionary

The use of a problem solving dictionary is a relatively simple strategy that can help a person develop skills that ultimately replace their problem behavior. A problem solving dictionary is simply a listing of the common situations that serve as contributing events or triggers for a person's behavior. These events can be described in the dictionary using pictures or words, depending on the needs of the individual. Next to each of these events is listed the appropriate response that should be used instead of the problem behavior. Once the list of events and appropriate responses has been developed, it should be kept in a day-planner or notebook so the person can carry it with them and have access to it no matter where they go.

The development of a problem solving dictionary, however, is only the first step. The second step is to ensure that the dictionary is reviewed with the person on a consistent basis. Once the person can describe the expected behavior, the third step is to practice the response. For example, if the problem solving dictionary lists "being called names" as the problem and "say to self *He is rude and I am not* and walk away" as the expected behavior, someone the individual trusts should act out this scenario with the individual.

This, of course, should only be undertaken with someone who can understand the concept that this is practice and who also consents to such practice.

I have found that the use of a problem solving dictionary is particularly effective for individuals diagnosed with Pervasive Developmental Disorders and those individuals who seem to take comfort in routines and rituals. For these individuals, the guidelines for expected behavior noted in the problem solving dictionary become the routine that must be followed. Thus, they are often driven to engage in the expected behavior rather than engage in the problem behavior. This strategy can also be very effective for individuals who are impulsive. The practicing of the expected behavior noted in the problem solving dictionary can, over time, become the behavior that is engaged in rather than the impulsive problem behavior.

Sensory Activities

Sensory dysfunction, or an inability to control or understand information coming from one's senses, may serve as a contributing or triggering event for problem behavior. Some individuals are very sensitive to stimulation and thus they may engage in problem behavior when they are over-stimulated. An example would be a person who regularly becomes upset when they are in a loud crowded room. Other individuals may have a high need for stimulation and may engage in problem behavior in an attempt to get their needs met. You might see this when a person becomes upset when you stop pushing his wheelchair because he likes the stimulation provided by movement.

As with everything else, a person's response to, and need for, stimulation is highly individualized. It is important to be familiar with the individual and his or her likes and dislikes. It is also important to observe the kinds of stimulation that are present, or absent, when the person displays problem behavior. Understanding a person's response to different stimulation gives us the best clues as to what kinds of interventions might be helpful. There are some generic activities that can be implemented if the person with problem behavior is having difficulty because of over or under-stimulation.

To help an over-stimulated person calm down, you can assist the person in participating in the following activities:

- Wrap-up in a heavy quilt
- Rock in a rocking chair or swing steadily
- Take a hot shower or bath
- Listen to slow or soft music
- Listen to calming sounds like ocean waves
- Dim the lights

If the person seems to be having difficulty because of under-stimulation, the following activities may be helpful:

- Sucking on sour ball or fireball candies (use only if there is no concern about possible choking)
- Applying a cold, wet washcloth to the face
- Lowering the temperature in the room
- Listening to quick paced/offbeat music
- Increasing the light in the room
- Listening to tapes/CDs of alerting nature sounds (birds)
- Taking a brisk walk

If the person with problem behavior seems to have more complicated sensory needs, you should probably contact an Occupational Therapist (OT) who has experience working with individuals with developmental disabilities. The benefit of collaborating with an OT is that these professionals can complete an individualized assessment and develop a "sensory diet" specific to the individual.

n Verbal Strategies

How we use our words can have a significant impact on whether an angry or agitated individual will engage in problem behavior. By using the strategies discussed next, we can communicate that we are sincerely interested in the person, are concerned about their problems, and are willing to help. When we communicate feelings such as these, we can often prevent problem behavior from occurring.

The first verbal strategy is exploring. **Exploring** involves encouraging the individual to further explain whatever it is they are trying to communicate.

An example of this is shown in the following scenario:

> **Jack:** "Everyone around here hates me!"
> **Tony:** "Tell me what happened."

Exploring

Exploring is often combined with another communication technique known as **validating.** Validating involves confirming the person's emotions while attempting to gain further information.

An example of this is shown in the following scenario:

> **Jack:** "Everybody around here hates me!"
> **Tony:** "It sounds as though you are pretty angry. What happened?"

Validating

Note that in the examples above, Tony did not challenge Jack's feelings or beliefs by telling Jack everyone likes him. Rather, Tony validated Jack's feeling and attempted to encourage Jack to further explain what made him feel this way. Challenging Jack's feelings (e.g., "No, Jack, everybody likes you.") would probably have led to more frustration (contributing event) and increased the chances for problem behavior.

Another useful strategy involves helping individuals to be in charge of themselves and the situation. One way we can do this it to verbally guide the individual through a problem solving process. You can assist someone in problem solving by:

Stating the problem or what the person seems to want

Assisting the person in identifying options to address the problem or help the person get what they want

Helping the person identify the consequences of each choice

Assisting the person in selecting a solution and helping them implement the solution

Problem Solving

Exploring, validating, and problem solving will help you develop a therapeutic relationship with others and thereby help prevent problem behavior. There are approaches, however, that are less effective and thus increase the chances of problem behavior.

Non-helpful reassurance is one such approach. Non-helpful reassurance occurs when we try to dispel the person's distress or worry by implying there is no reason for it. Doing this devalues the person's feelings and communicates a lack of understanding and empathy. This can then create an emotional reaction in the person that can contribute to or trigger problem behavior.

An example of **non-helpful reassurance** is included in the next scenario:

> Jack: "I am really worried about my mother."
> Tony: "I wouldn't worry about her. She's fine."

Non-helpful reassurance

Another way we can inhibit the development of a therapeutic relationship and increase the chances of problem behavior is by **changing the subject** when someone is trying to talk to us about something. When we do this, it takes control away from the individual and communicates we do not think what they have to say is important.

An example of this is included in the next scenario:

Jack: "I want to go to the store!"
Tony: "Didn't you play basketball today."

Changing the subject

Finally, another common thing we do to interfere with the development of a therapeutic relationship is to **belittle or minimize other's feelings**.

An example of this is included in the next scenario:

Jack: "I am so sad. I almost feel like killing myself."
Tony: "Everybody feels sad."

Belittle or minimize other's feelings

By ensuring that we consistently use *validating* and *exploring* statements, and avoid *non-helpful reassurance, minimization,* and *subject changing,* we can better establish a therapeutic relationship with others. In addition, we are able defuse situations that might otherwise evolve into problem behavior.

De-escalation Strategies

Sometimes, no matter what we do, individuals will become angry or threatening. When a person becomes upset, there are some general rules we should try to follow. These rules address the areas of personal space (*proxemics*), body posture *(kinesics)*, and word delivery. By paying attention to where our bodies are in space, to our posture and movement, and to how we deliver our words, we can avoid accidentally engaging in behavior that could serve as a trigger for problem behavior. Things to keep in mind include:

Personal Space
- Keep at least three feet between yourself and the person
- Do not move closer to the person unless necessary to protect others from harm
- If a person gets close to you, slowly and carefully back-up
- When possible, put an object (e.g., table) between yourself and the person

Body Posture
- Do not make strong gestures (e.g., pointing)
- Keep movements slow and predictable
- Do not stand face-to-face
- Stand at forty-five degree angle to the person
- Do not make intense eye-contact

Word Delivery
- Keep tone of voice normal
- Use normal volume
- Use fewer words
- Use simplest language possible
- Talk slower than normal

Once the situation has been resolved, it is time to go back and, using the ABC Tracksheets, try to determine the contributing and triggering events. This will help in planning ways to prevent the situation in the future.

Implementation and Monitoring for Effectiveness

Although this manual was not designed to teach you to conduct behavioral assessments and write formal behavioral support plans, it is still important to ensure any chosen interventions are included in an individual's PCP, IHP and/or ISP. It is also important to ensure that a plan to ensure consistent implementation is developed and communicated to all those involved. In addition, it is critical to ensure that any chosen support strategy is consistent with the values, skills, and resources of the individuals who will be asked to implement it. No one should ever be asked to implement a support strategy in which they do not believe, or one that they do not have the time to consistently implement.

In order to assess the effects of any implemented support strategies, data collection strategies must be implemented. The ABC Tracksheet described earlier can be helpful in determining whether the supports we implement are effective in reducing the frequency and/or intensity of a person's problem behavior. Data from the ABC Tracksheets (e.g., frequency of problem behaviors) from before our interventions were implemented should be compared with ABC Tracksheets from after our interventions were implemented. This will help us to determine if our efforts have been successful. Regardless of whether ABC tracksheets or some other documentation system is used, it is critical to ensure a documentation system is in place, and consistently utilized, so we can assess the effectiveness of our interventions. If we believe the strategies we have implemented are not bringing about the desired effect or are making things worse, additional assessments and/or changes in support strategies should be undertaken.

Finally, it is important to remember that consent must be obtained from the individual and their legally responsible person, if applicable, prior to implementing any supports designed to decrease problem behavior.

In Closing

It has been my experience that some of the most common outcomes of working or living with individuals with problem behavior are stress, frustration, and a sense of helplessness. Because these feelings are practically unavoidable, it is important for us to develop ways to cope with these feelings before they become contributing or triggering events for our own problem behavior.

Fortunately, now that you have read this book you know a variety of ways to help others, and yourself, deal with stress, anxiety, and frustration. It is my sincere hope that you will include in your life some of the strategies we have reviewed. After all, who among us could not benefit from more frequent mood-enhancing activities, better sleep, more exercise, and so on. It is also my sincere hope that through the use of these strategies, you will have the strength and energy to continue supporting the individuals who were the motivation for your reading of this book.

In closing, I will leave you with a quote I often reflect upon as I struggle to make a positive difference in the lives of others.

Give what you have. To someone, it may be better than you dare think.

Henry Wadsworth Longfellow

APPENDIX A

BEHAVIORAL EQUIVALENTS FOR SOME DSM-IV DISORDERS

SCHIZOPHRENIA

DSM-IV Symptom	Possible Presentation in Individual with Mental Retardation (Myers and Peuschel, 1993; Ryan 1996)
Delusion	<ul><li>New avoidance or fear behaviors</li><li>Irrational beliefs not previously expressed</li><li>Bizarre accusations regarding others</li><li>Sudden refusal to take medications (i.e., belief medication is poison)</li><li>Carefully inspecting food as if it has been tampered with</li></ul>
Hallucination	<ul><li>Talking to non-existent people</li><li>Turning head as if listening to sounds no one else hears</li><li>Reporting on conversations not heard by others</li><li>Sniffing air as if smelling something not smelled by others</li><li>Pushing unseen objects off of body</li><li>Covering eyes or ears as if to block out hallucinations</li><li>Sudden appearance of "shadow boxing"</li></ul>
Disorganized Speech	<ul><li>Regression in language skills</li><li>Decrease in amount of language</li><li>Speech no longer makes sense</li></ul>
Grossly Disorganized or Catatonic Behavior	<ul><li>Sudden appearance of new unusual mannerisms</li><li>Assuming the same position for long periods</li><li>Regression in performance of previously acquired skills</li></ul>
Negative Symptoms	<ul><li>Lack of expression of emotions (must represent a change from baseline)</li><li>Lack of interest in previously enjoyed activities</li><li>Reinforcers no longer effective</li><li>Speech no longer present</li></ul>

MAJOR DEPRESSION

<u>DSM-IV Symptom</u>　　　　　　　　<u>Possible Presentation in Someone with Retardation</u> (Sovner & Lowry, 1990; Ryan, 1996, Lowry, 1995)

Depressed Mood

- Frequent unexplained crying
- Decrease in laughter and smiling
- General irritability and subsequent aggression or self-injury
- Sad facial expression

Loss of Interest in Pleasure

- No longer participates in favorite activities
- Reinforcers no longer valued
- Increased time spent in room alone
- Refusals of most work/social activities

**Weight Change/
Appetite Change**

- Measured weight changes
- Increased refusals to come to table to eat
- Unusually disruptive at meal times
- Constant food seeking behaviors

Insomnia

- Disruptive at bed time
- Repeatedly gets up at night
- Difficulty falling asleep
- No longer gets up for work/activities
- Early morning awakening

Hypersomnia

- Over 12 hours of sleep per day
- Naps frequently

Psychomotor Agitation

- Restlessness/Fidgety
- Pacing
- Increased disruptive behavior

MAJOR DEPRESSION CONTINUED

Psychomotor Retardation

- Sits for extended periods of time
- Moves slowly
- Takes longer than usual to complete activities

Fatigue/Loss of Energy

- Needs frequent breaks to complete simple activity
- Slumped/Tired body posture
- Does not complete tasks with multiple steps

Feelings of Worthlessness

- Statements like "I'm dumb", "I'm retarded", etc.
- Seeming to seek punishment
- Social isolation

Lack of Concentration

- Decreased work output in vocational setting
- Does not stay with tasks to completion
- Decrease in IQ upon retesting

Thoughts of Death

- Preoccupation with family member's deaths (e.g., increased interest in visiting grave, carrying photographs of deceased relatives, etc.)
- Talking about committing/attempting suicide
- Fascination with violent movies/television shows

BIPOLAR DISORDER

<u>DSM IV Symptoms</u>　　　　　<u>Possible Presentation in Someone with Mental Retardation</u>
　　　　　　　　　　　　　　　(Sovner & Lowry, 1990; Ryan, 1996, Lowry, 1997)

Euphoric, Elevated or Irritable Mood

- Smiling, hugging or being affectionate with people who previously were not favored by the individual
- Slapping at previously favored person (i.e., irritable mood)
- Boisterousness
- Over-reactivity to small incidents
- Extreme excitement
- Excessive laughing and giggling
- Self-injury associated with irritability
- Enthusiastic greeting of everyone

Decreased Need for Sleep

- Behavioral challenges when prompted to go to bed
- Constantly getting up at night
- Seems rested after not sleeping (i.e., not irritable due to lack of sleep as is common in depression)
- Works on activities in room during the night

Inflated Self-Esteem/ Grandiosity

- Making improbable claims (e.g., is a staff member, has mastered all necessary skills, etc.)
- Wearing excessive make-up
- Dressing provocatively
- Demanding rewards

Flight of Ideas

- Disorganized speech
- Thoughts not connected
- Quickly changing subjects

BIPOLAR DISORDER CONTINUED

**More Talkative/
Pressured Speech**

- Increased singing
- Increased swearing
- Perseverative speech
- Screaming
- Intruding in order to say something
- Non-verbal communication increases
- Increase in vocalizations

Distractibility

- Decrease in work/task performance
- Leaving tasks uncompleted
- Inability to sit through activities (e.g., favorite tv show)

**Agitation/Increase in
Goal Directed Behavior**

- Pacing
- Negativism
- Working on many activities at once
- Fidgeting
- Aggression
- Rarely sits

**Excessive Pleasurable
Activities**

- Increase in masturbation
- Sexualizing previously platonic relationships
- Teasing others
- Giving away/spending money

BORDERLINE PERSONALITY DISORDER

<u>DSM IV Symptoms</u>　　　　<u>Possible Presentation in Someone with Mental Retardation</u>
(DesNoyers Hurley, & Sovner, 1990; Moses, 1999):

Personal Relationships

- Relationships are volatile
- Individual grossly overreacts to staff requests
- Use of disturbing slurs against others
- Becomes over-attached to a person and then "turns against" them for no obvious reason
- Over idealization of staff or significant others

Impulsivity

- Provoking others
- Dangerous sexual activity
- Substance abuse
- Stealing
- Binge eating

Mood Instability

- Extreme change in mood due to minor or nonexistent issue

Poor Anger Control

- Verbal aggression (most frequently)
- Physical aggression

Suicidal/Self Injurious Beh.

- Cutting self with sharp objects
- Attempts at suicide

Fear of Abandonment

- Repeatedly calling staff/family member on phone (e.g., 10-20 times a day)
- Dramatic acts designed to keep person from leaving
- Unreasonable demands of staff time
- Acts designed to "get rid of" others so as not to have to live in fear that they may be abandoned

Identity Disturbance

- Confused or shifting sexual identity
- Stating a person is someone other than who they are

BORDERLINE PERSONALITY DISORDER CONTINUED

Paranoid/Disassociative Symptoms

- Statements about others "out to get them"
- Avoidance behaviors
- Bizarre accusations regarding staff
- Non-seizure/neurological periods of confused consciousness

APPENDIX B

TRACKING SHEETS

SLEEP SHEET

Name: _____

Dates:								

KEY: **A** = awake   **S** = sleep   **U** = Unknown

Time								
12:00 am								
12:30 am								
1:00 am								
1:30 am								
2:00 am								
2:30 am								
3:00 am								
3:30 am								
4:00 am								
4:30 am								
5:00 am								
5:30 am								
6:00 am								
6:30 am								
7:00 am								
7:30 am								
8:00 am								
8:30 am								
9:00 am								
9:30 am								
10:00 am								
10:30 am								
11:00 am								
11:30 am								
12:00 pm								
12:30 pm								
1:00 pm								
1:30 pm								
2:00 pm								
2:30 pm								
3:00 pm								
3:30 pm								
4:00 pm								
4:30 pm								
5:00 pm								
5:30 pm								
6:00 pm								
6:30 pm								
7:00 pm								
7:30 pm								
8:00 pm								
8:30 pm								
9:00 pm								
9:30 pm								
10:00 pm								
10:30 pm								
11:00 pm								
11:30 pm								

A.B.C. Tracksheet

Name:_____   Date:_____

Time:_____   Place:_____

Antecedents	**Behaviors**	**Consequences**

Name of Person Completing Form:_____

APPENDIX C

SELF MONITORING AND BEHAVIORAL CONTRACTS

Self-Monitoring

Self-Monitoring at Work

Date: _____

Select 3 Jobs	Job Choices	Jobs Completed
_____	Clean up after lunch	_____
_____	Clean bathrooms	_____
_____	Mop floors	_____
_____	Take out trash	_____
_____	Sweep floors	_____

Walked away from others when teased	YES	NO
Told Boss	YES	NO

Self-Monitoring

Riding the Bus Skills

Date: _____

	YES	NO
I stood at the bus stop	____	____
I did not talk to strangers	____	____
I did not touch strangers	____	____
I got on bus #309	____	____
I said "hello" to the bus driver	____	____
I put my money in the correct slot	____	____
I sat in an empty seat	____	____
I stayed seated until the bus stopped at my stop	____	____
I said "good-bye" to the bus driver	____	____

Self-Monitoring

DATE
_____

DATE
_____

Behavior Contract

Effective Dates: From: _____ to _____

David agrees to get along with others at work. He also agrees when others at work try to make him lose his temper he will:

- Tell Them to "Stop it, I don't like when you do that."
- Walk Away
- Tell his Boss
- Tell Himself "I did the right thing."

Reinforcer: 25 points every time David tells others to stop, walks away, tells his supervisor, and tells himself "I did the right thing."

Penalty: David will lose 50 points for each incident of hitting others.

_____   _____
David   Job Coach

Behavior Contract

DATE:_____

NO

YES

___ ___ ___

References

Barry, L. & Messer, J. (2003). A practical application of self-management for students diagnosed with attention-deficit hyperactivity disorder. *Journal of Positive Behavioral Interventions.* 5(3): 238-248.

Carr, E.G., McLaughlin, D.M., Giacobbe-Grieco, T., & Smith, C.E.. (2003). Using mood rating and mood induction in assessment andintervention for severe problem behavior. *American Journal on Mental Retardation,* 108(1): 32-55.

DesNoyers Hurley, A. & Sovner, R. (1988). The clinical characteristics and management of borderline personality disorder in mentally retarded persons. *Psychiatric Aspects of Mental Retardation Reviews,* 7, 7-8.

Gardner, W.I., Griffiths, D., & Nugent J. (1999). *Behavioral supports: Individual centered interventions – A multimodal functional approach.* Kingston, NY: NADD Press.

Gerdner, L.A. (2000). Effects of individualized versus classical "relaxation" music on the frequency of agitation in elderly persons with alzheimer's disease and related disorders. *International Psychogeriatrics.* 12(1): 49-65.

Hadfield, N. (2001). The role of aromatherapy in reducing anxiety in patients with malignant brain tumors. *International Journal of Palliative Nursing,* 7(6):279-85.

Lowry, M.A. (1995). Anger: A root of problem behavior in the depressed. *The Habilitative Mental Healthcare Newsletter.* 14(6).

Lowry, M.A. (1997). Unmasking mood disorders: Recognizing and measuring symptomatic behavior. *The Habilitative Mental Healthcare Newsletter.* 16(1).

Myers, B.A. & Peuschel, S.M. (1993). Differentiating schizophrenia from other mental disorders and behavioral disorders in persons with developmental disabilities. *The Habilitative Mental Healthcare Newsletter,* 12(6).

Preston, J.D. (2001). *Lift your mood now.* Oakland, CA: New Harbinger Press.

Ryan, R. (1999). *Handbook of mental health care for persons with developmental disabilities.* Evergreen, CO:. S&B Publishing.

Smallwood, J. (2001). Aromotherapy and behavior disturbances in dementia: A randomized controlled trial. *International Journal of Geriatric Psychiatry,* 16(10):1010-3.

Sovner, R. & Lowry, M.A. (1990). A behavioral methodology for diagnosing affective disorders in individuals with mental retardation. *The Habilitiative Mental Healthcare Newsletter*, 9(7).

Stamatelos, T. & Mott, D. (1985). Creative potentional among those labeled developmentally delayed. *The Arts in Psychotherapy*, 12, 101-113.